THE POWER OF A
PRAYING NATION

Don Nori

Treasure House
An Imprint of
Destiny Image® Publishers, Inc.
P.O. Box 310
Shippensburg, PA 17257-0310

"For where your treasure is, there will your heart be also."
Matthew 6:21

ISBN 0-7684-3045-3

For Worldwide Distribution
Printed in the U.S.A.

This book and all other Destiny Image, Revival Press, MercyPlace, Fresh Bread, Destiny Image Fiction, and Treasure House books, available everywhere books are sold worldwide.

For a U.S. bookstore nearest you, call **1-800-722-6774.**
For more information on foreign distributors, call **717-532-3040.**
Or reach us on the Internet: **www.destinyimage.com**

Dedication

This book is dedicated to all the innocent victims of the terrorist attacks perpetrated against the United States on September 11, 2001.

To the survivors, whose lives are forever changed.

To the memory of the deceased, and to their families and friends, who now must learn to live without them.

May God strengthen you and keep you.

May His Presence comfort you.

May His love give you hope.

Please Note:

For the first year, the author is donating all royalties from the sale of this book to the relief efforts of the September 11, 2001 terrorist attacks.

Acknowledgments

Without the organization of Elizabeth Allen;
the inspiration of Don Nori Jr.;
the "out-of-the-box" thinking of Jeff Milam;
the creativity of Jeff Hall;
the administrative work of Dian Layton;
the research of Heritage Fellowship;
the content assistance of Don Milam, Pastor Cleddie
Keith, and Charles Slagle;
you would not be holding this book in your hands.

"Thank you" is not enough.

From the Desk of the Publisher

"We will get through this."

Many people were involved in putting this book together. It was truly a work of love and devotion for this nation and fellow Americans. It was a fulfilling assignment during this most difficult time. As publishers, we feel a very deep responsibility to provide literature that will encourage, inspire, and remind all Americans just who we are and what we stand for as a people. We will get through this. We will do more than survive. We will grow through this. We will grow in love toward one another and in our love toward God. We will emerge many times the leaders we were before this atrocity occurred. We have the will and we have the faith. We have the commitment to family and nation, and we are coming together in a way that makes us a more formidable foe than ever before in our history. With the greatest conviction and with the greatest pride, with more respect and more love than most of us have ever experienced — today we declare as one people, "God Bless America."

Contributing Authors

Cleddie Keith

Pastor Cleddie Keith is a man consumed with a passion for revival. For the past 20 years, he has served as senior pastor of Heritage Fellowship, located in the greater Cincinnati area. Pastor Keith is a pastor's pastor. He speaks in countless meetings and conferences. Under his leadership, ministries have been birthed around the world. The heart of his message is to hear what the Lord is saying to the Church, and to spur pastors on to contend for true revival.

Dian Layton

Dian has a heart for the nations and for the generations. She has ministered internationally in a wide variety of settings for over 15 years. Dian is the author of *Soldiers With Little Feet*; *Hinds' Feet on High Places* (illustrated version for children); *The Young God Chasers* children's church curriculum, and the *Adventures in the Kingdom*™ children's series.

Don Milam Jr.

Don Milam is the Acquisitions Editor at Destiny Image Publishers. He and his wife, Micki, have had an amazing journey: working with drug addicts both in Philadelphia, Pennsylvania and in Maputo, Mozambique, East Africa; imprisonment under a communist regime; pastoring churches; and most importantly, raising a daughter and two sons. Don is the author of *The Lost Passions of Jesus* and numerous articles that can be read at Destiny Image's website: www.reapernet.com

Charles Slagle

For over 30 years, via their traveling ministry throughout the world, Charles Slagle and his wife, Paula, have led many people to Christ. Notorious for their refreshingly nonreligious approach, they have a passion to reveal God's true character and dismantle bogus traditions that barricade hope from needy people. Charles has written three books: *From the Father's Heart*, *Power to Soar*, and *Invitation to Friendship: From the Father's Heart, Vol. 2.*

Contents

SECTION ONE

A PRAYING NATION

Don Nori

Psalm 23

A psalm of strength and hope.
A psalm of David.

The Lord is my shepherd; I shall not want
He maketh me to lie down in green pastures:
He leadeth me beside the still waters
He restoreth my soul:
He leadeth me in the paths of righteousness
for His name's sake.
Yea, though I walk through the valley
of the shadow of death,
I will fear no evil:
for Thou art with me;
Thy rod and Thy staff they comfort me
Thou preparest a table before me
in the presence of mine enemies:
Thou anointest my head with oil;
my cup runneth over
Surely goodness and mercy
shall follow me all the days of my life:
and I will dwell in the house of the Lord for ever.

CHAPTER ONE

Blessed Is the Nation Whose God Is the Lord

(Psalm 33:12).

A PRAYING NATION IS A POWERFUL NATION. She has confidence and assurance that is unparalleled among the world's community of states. Often misunderstood as arrogance, this power is proven divine by her generosity and humility toward the rest of the world.

Her power does not rest in her armies or in her military hardware. Her power is not measured by her economic accomplishments or her technological advances. Her power rests in her prayers and in the One to whom she prays. In quiet confidence and assurance, her hidden strength is in an all-powerful God. It must be that one becomes like the One to whom he prays, bearing all the strengths and power of the deity in which he has trusted. There is no question about it. A praying nation is a powerful nation.

A PRAYING NATION IS A LOVING NATION. Our security was woven into the very fabric of who we are as a people. In spite of how some would attempt to rewrite our history, our forefathers established this country on the eternal principles of prayer and faith toward God. Had security not been established at our beginnings, it would be as illusive as it is to so many nations today. No, we cannot make this a secure nation—we can only protect and preserve the security that is a foundational building block of our history. Such security is not based in words but in confidence in God Himself.

Our nation is protected by a power much greater than any human words can define, for that would require the ability to understand the greatness of His power to begin with. His reign is above all and carries with it the most formidable resolve that eternity can muster.

Angels hover over a praying nation. They protect her and watch over her children. They are alert and attentive to all her enemies, ready in a moment to protect her from all harm.

The nation that prays has a security that cannot be matched in the universe. There are no armies, no strategies, no plans that can overpower the strength of a praying nation. For her wisdom is born from above, and the courage to carry out that wisdom comes from above.

Her edge is her faith in an unseen realm, where God alone rules and the affairs of man are dictated by a force born of human faith, and heavenly resolve. A praying nation causes Heaven itself to shatter time and space, replacing the vile and the hideous with the purposes of God.

King David ruled over a praying nation. The very existence of that people depended solely upon the relationship between that nation and the God who covered and protected it.

King David's Psalm 121 tells us of the understanding and trust he discovered as he prayed to his Lord in the most brutal of circumstances.

I will lift up mine eyes unto the hills, from whence cometh my help.

My help cometh from the Lord, which made heaven and earth.

He will not suffer thy foot to be moved: He that keeps thee will not slumber.

Behold, He that keepeth Israel shall neither slumber nor sleep.

The Lord is thy keeper: the Lord is thy shade upon thy right hand.

The sun shall not smite thee by day, nor the moon by night.

The Lord shall preserve thee from all evil: He shall preserve thy soul.

The Lord shall preserve thy going out and thy coming in from this time forth, and even for evermore.

A PRAYING NATION IS A SECURE NATION. Because she is loving, she is by nature compassionate and patient. Never mistake her patience for weakness, for it is her love that causes her to hope for the impossible and believe the best when there is no basis for it.

Love causes her to lay aside the differences she has with others in the face of human disaster and misery. A loving nation clothes and feeds even her enemies in times of distress. She opposes cruelty and injustice even when it is brought to her foes.

A loving nation exercises patience in all things and does not allow her anger to be kindled easily. But do not mistake her anger for fear, for she is aware of the troubles of the world. She will hope until life itself is threatened, before rising in holy anger and righteous indignation.

A loving nation responds to the needs around her. She cannot turn a deaf ear or a blind eye to suffering of any kind. A praying nation is a loving nation.

A PRAYING NATION IS A HOLY NATION. She understands that her holy words to a holy God are not separate from her unholy actions. She walks softly before her Lord, with reverence and godly fear. She does not presume upon His kindness or demand His attention. A holy nation knows precisely her place in the grand scheme of things and has no desire to change places with Him.

Her life is one of quiet repentance, daily confessing her faults as individual citizens and as a nation. She cries to God for mercy and forgiveness, fully confident that whoever repents of his sin to the Lord is forgiven. This confessed sin is summarily cast into the sea of forgetfulness, never to torment her again with its blazing guilt and haunting memory.

She knows that God loves her. She knows His hand is stretched out to her in loving strength and comfort. Her weakness keeps her humble and her love keeps her at His breast in relentless prayer for strength to overcome the sin that seems to befall her so easily.

She is all too aware of her humanity. Her strength is in knowing her weakness; her humility is visible in the cry to the Lord for His strength; her future is in His mercy; her power is in her prayer. A praying nation is a holy nation.

How blessed are the people who live this way!
How blessed are the people whose God is the Lord!
(See Psalm 144: 15.)

CHAPTER TWO

God Loves Us

WHY DOES IT SEEM SO HARD FOR US TO UNDERSTAND and accept how much God loves us? We were on His mind long before the world came into being. He created us for His pleasure. He gave us His only Son to forgive us and His Holy Spirit to gather us to Himself.

Sometimes it seems we try so hard to figure out the things that are difficult to grasp, that we forget the things that are so simple.

God loves us. That is simple. Jesus said it. Look at John 15:9 and 13. "As the Father has loved me, so have I loved you...Greater love has no man than this, that a man lay down his life for his friends."

He cares for us so much more than we can ever imagine. He is constantly with us. In fact, God is so big that He gives His full attention to each one of us individually. That is amazing! He is so big that He focuses on each one of us personally. He knows us intimately. He knows our struggles and our pain. He knows our fears and our sorrows.

He also knows our hopes and our dreams. He knows the deepest desires of our hearts and He knows how all those things work together to make us who we are and to make all our dreams come true.

There now, it is not so complicated after all. We may not be able to understand ourselves, but there is One who not only understands, but also made us the way we are for a specific purpose. We are not complicated to God. He loves us personally, totally, passionately. He cares for us and is striving with us to bring all our dreams into reality.

GOD LOVES YOU. Some people think that the more important you are, the more God will love you. That just is not true. He does not care more for the rich or the famous. He does not love some people more than others. He does not think that some are not worth His love.

He loves us all, no matter what we have done or how far we think we have strayed from Him. His love is much bigger than our sin and more powerful than our guilt. Always remember that God loves who we are. His deepest desire is toward His creation. He will always strive with us, drawing us to Himself.

To try to understand why bad things happen is more than most of us can bear. But we do know that God loves us. This is what we should center our thoughts on, since He is really our only source of comfort. We know that He created us to be just like Him. Long before you were born, God knew you—and knowing you, He loved you. The world can be cruel at times to turn away from us, but we must never forget how much God loves us.

Some people think that they have sinned too much or have ignored Him for too long. They think that God is just like we are. They think He holds grudges and remembers our failures. But God loves us. He is a forgiving God. He is easy to talk to and is anxious to forgive us. All we need to do is ask Him. After all, He loved us so much that He sent His only Son, Jesus, to die in our place. Jesus took all our sins with Him when He went to the cross. When He died, He took all our sins with Him into hell. When He rose from the dead three days later, He left our sins in hell, so they would never be able to make us feel guilty again.

He waits for us to ask Him to forgive us. He waits for us to ask Him to take the sins we have committed and to set us free from the guilt we feel for what we have done.

Oh how deeply God loves us! We must never be afraid of Him. We must never feel that He wants to punish us. The Lord Jesus took our punishment so we could feel God's love and experience the blessings of belonging to Him.

God loves *you* and is waiting for you to come to Him.

Chapter Three

God Loves America

IF WE ARE GOING TO ASK GOD TO FIGHT FOR US and protect us, we need to clearly understand that God really does love America

If we are not certain that we are loved, how will we ever have the faith to believe that He will answer our prayers? How will we ever have the courage and assurance to approach Him?

I know God loves America for several reasons:

1. AMERICA HAS PROVIDED AN ATMOSPHERE OF FREEDOM and peace that has allowed us to grow in faith and in numbers. There is the precious element of freedom that

allows Christians to share their faith personally and broadcast their faith in whatever medium they choose. As a result of this freedom, the gospel is preached over television and radio. It is published in tens of thousands of Internet sites as well as in newspapers and magazines. We record countless CDs with the gospel message and even make movies that preach the gospel. God loves a nation where His people can freely declare their faith and love to Him.

Blessed is the nation whose God is the Lord...the people whom He has chosen for His own inheritance. (Psalm 33:12).

Yes, I know there are threats to that freedom. I know that there are those who want to silence the gospel—that is for another book. Today it is important to know that God loves America first and foremost because there is freedom of worship and assembly, freedom of expression and declaration.

2. THERE HAS NEVER BEEN A MORE GENEROUS NATION on the planet than America. We have opened our hearts and our hands and our pocketbooks to the needs of the world. We have compassion and true love for our fellow human beings. We have rebuilt cities after natural disasters and rebuilt nations after wars. Even when the nations who needed help were the nations we had defeated in war, our hearts reached to them and gave generously. The United States has been first in fulfilling the chosen fast that the Lord said was the true fast in Isaiah 58:6-7.

Is not this the fast that I have chosen? to loose the bands of wickedness, to undo the heavy burdens, and to let the oppressed go free, and that ye break every yoke? Is it not to deal thy bread to the hungry, and that thou bring the poor that are cast out to thy house? when thou seest the naked, that thou cover him; and that thou hide not thyself from thine own flesh? (Isaiah 58:6-7).

America's generosity has made her a great nation, blessed of the Lord and loved by Him. For God loves a nation that loves the world and is willing to care for it to the best of her ability. God loves America.

The liberal soul shall be made fat: and he that watereth shall be watered also himself. (Proverbs 11:25).

3. **AMERICA HAS NEVER BEEN ABLE TO STAND BY IDLY** in the face of oppression around the world. Man may criticize us for our intervention when totalitarianism threatens other nations. But God loves us for it. We have put ourselves at risk for the sake of freedom-loving peoples around the world. We have stood against the bullies of the world and fought for the same freedoms that we ourselves have come to cherish.

For the Lord loveth judgment, and forsaketh not his saints; they are preserved for ever: but the seed of the wicked shall be cut off (Psalm 37:28).

Yes, God loves America. He wants her to continue to be a light to the nations; an example of true love to the

Lord and our fellowman; an example of selfless giving and compassion to all the needy and destitute of the world.

His plan for America is far from over. It is far from complete. We must not allow ourselves to give into fear and uncertainty. Rather, let us go before the Lord with confidence and faith. He loves our land, for He loves those who dwell within her borders.

CHAPTER FOUR

God Wants to Answer Our Prayers

THIS MAY BE A NEW THOUGHT TO SOME PEOPLE, but God really does want to answer our prayers. He does not have to be begged. He does not have to be convinced of our motives, for He knows our hearts better than we do.

God wants more than anything else to give us what we ask for. In fact, He wants to give us more than we could ask or think or even imagine.

The Scriptures speak often about how much God wants to answer our prayers. One of my favorite passages is in the Gospel of Matthew:

Ask, and it shall be given you; seek, and ye shall find; knock, and it shall be opened unto you. For every one that asks receives; and he that seeks finds; and to him that knocks it shall be opened. What man is there of you, whom if his son ask bread, will he give him a stone? Or if he ask a fish, will he give him a serpent? If you then, being evil, know how to give good gifts unto your children, how much more shall your Father which is in heaven give good things to them that ask Him? (See Matthew 7:7-11.)

Here are some other wonderful Bible promises to think about:

And it shall come to pass, that before they call, I will answer; and while they are yet speaking, I will hear (Isaiah 65: 24).

If ye abide in Me, and My words abide in you, ye shall ask what ye will, and it shall be done unto you (John 15:7).

And Jesus said unto them, Have faith in God. For truly I say unto you, That whosoever shall say unto this mountain, Be removed, and be cast into the sea; and shall not doubt in his heart, but shall believe that those things which he says shall come to pass; he shall have whatsoever he says. Therefore I say unto you, What things you desire, when you pray, believe that you receive them, and you shall have them. (See Mark 11:22-24.)

GOD IS A GOOD GOD. He loves us and wants to care for all our needs because He loves us so completely.

People often feel that God does not care or that He will not answer our prayers because He is too busy with other things. Some people think they are not important enough for the Lord to listen to their needs and their problems. I have discovered something very important about why we do not believe that He wants to bless us and take of us.

We often feel unworthy because our lives are not what they should be or what they could be. We believe that we have sinned; therefore, God hates us—or at least He will ignore us when we are in need.

Well, nothing is more hopeless than this kind of belief. If we cannot turn to God for help and comfort, who *can* we turn to? He is the most forgiving, the most loving, the most compassionate One in all the universe.

GOD KNOWS OUR STRUGGLES. He knows our sin. The power of a praying nation begins with the power of repentance. We can run to Him any time. He forgives our sins and leads us into the right way of doing things.

He wants to answer our prayers no matter how insignificant we think they may be. He deals with the sin problems immediately so He can help us in our times of need.

From God's point of view, His arms are open to us and His love is always extended to His creation. He is always calling us to Himself.

From our point of view, we feel there are things that will keep us from praying effectively. We have trouble believing that God cares and will really answer our prayers.

King David felt the same way when he was caught in sin with a soldier's wife and subsequently had the soldier killed to hide his sin. Now there was a man in trouble. Yet King David understood enough about God to know he should run *to* Him and not *away from* Him. He knew God wanted to answer his prayers, so He simply repented to the God he loved and who loved him.

Here is the king's prayer. Maybe you want to pray this prayer too.

Have mercy upon me, O God, according to Thy lovingkindness: according to the multitude of Thy tender mercies. Blot out my transgressions.

Wash me thoroughly from mine iniquity, and cleanse me from my sin.

For I acknowledge my transgressions: and my sin is ever before me.

Against Thee, Thee only, have I sinned, and done this evil in Thy sight....

Behold, You want truth in the inward parts: and in the hidden part Thou shalt make me to know wisdom.

Purge me, and I shall be clean: wash me, and I shall be whiter than snow.

Make me to hear joy and gladness; that the bones which Thou hast broken may rejoice.

Hide Thy face from my sins, and blot out all mine iniquities.

Create in me a clean heart, O God; and renew a right spirit within me.

Cast me not away from Thy Presence; and take not Thy holy spirit from me.

Restore unto me the joy of Thy salvation; and uphold me with Thy free spirit.

Then will I teach transgressors Thy ways; and sinners shall be converted unto Thee.

Deliver me from bloodguiltiness, O God, Thou God of my salvation: and my tongue shall sing aloud of Thy righteousness.

O Lord, open Thou my lips; and my mouth shall show forth Thy praise.

For Thou desirest not sacrifice; else would I give it: You do not delight in my good works.

The sacrifices of God are a broken spirit: a broken and a contrite heart, O God, Thou wilt not despise.
(See Psalm 51:1-17.)

Now praying that prayer from your heart to the Lord Jesus takes away the guilt of your sin. You can know with confidence that He loves you and wants to answer your prayers.

We can learn a lot from King David. Even though he had sinned so terribly, he could still experience God's love and power in his life. King David was not afraid to ask the Lord for anything, because he knew God loved him and wanted to answer his prayers.

Here are some prayers that King David prayed after he asked God to forgive him. He was a man who understood that he really was free from the guilt of his sin

Psalms of David.

Let God arise, let His enemies be scattered: let them also that hate Him flee before Him.

As smoke is driven away, so drive them away: as wax melteth before the fire, so let the wicked perish at the Presence of God.

But let the righteous be glad; let them rejoice before God: yea, let them exceedingly rejoice **(Psalm 68:1-3).**

Give ear, O Lord, unto my prayer; and attend to the voice of my supplications.

In the day of my trouble I will call upon Thee: for Thou wilt answer me.

Among the gods there is none like unto Thee, O Lord; neither are there any works like unto Thy works.

All nations whom Thou hast made shall come and worship before Thee, O Lord; and shall glorify Thy name.

For Thou art great, and doest wondrous things: Thou art God alone.

Teach me Thy way, O Lord; I will walk in Thy truth: unite my heart to fear Thy name **(Psalm 86:6-11).**

HISTORY PROVES THE POWER OF PRAYER

Don Milam Jr.

Psalm 64

A psalm of King David when he prayed for
protection and destruction of the enemy.

Hear my voice, O God, in my prayer:
preserve my life from fear of the enemy.
Hide me from the secret counsel of the wicked;
from the insurrection of the workers of iniquity:
Who whet their tongue like a sword, and bend their
bows to shoot their arrows, even bitter words:
That they may shoot in secret at the perfect:
suddenly do they shoot at him, and fear not.
They encourage themselves in an evil matter:
they commune of laying snares privily; they say,
Who shall see them? They search out iniquities;
they accomplish a diligent search: both the inward
thought of every one of them, and the heart, is deep.
But God shall shoot at them with an arrow;
suddenly shall they be wounded. So they shall make
their own tongue to fall upon themselves: all that see
them shall flee away. And all men shall fear, and shall
declare the work of God; for they shall wisely consider
of his doing. The righteous shall be glad in the
LORD, and shall trust in him;
and all the upright in heart shall glory.

History Proves the Power of Prayer

Praying, for many people, is more of a private practice than a public exercise. Therefore, it is difficult to trace and gather together a collection of prayers prayed by famous people. Fortunately, some of those prayers have found their way to the printed page so that we can now make them available to you.

Some may ask, "Why publish the prayers of others?" That is a good question that deserves a relevant answer.

First, as we meditate on the richness of their meaning, the prayers of others can deepen our own reflections in the midst of sorrowful and demanding situations.

Second, when we are anesthetized by the pain of loss or the pressure of life we often cannot find the right words to express ourselves to God. The prayers of others can provide those words.

Third, the prayers of famous people will reveal to us how these men and women whom we admire have turned to God in prayer in the midst of their own trying circumstances.

Coupled with the prayers of some of the great leaders of the past we have sprinkled in reflections by some of the founding fathers of this great nation. As a praying nation, it is good to be reminded of the religious convictions of our forefathers.

We offer this collection of prayers and reflections as a source of solace and a means for meditation.

Mother Teresa – Missionary of Compassion, 20th Century

Dear Jesus, help us to spread your fragrance everywhere we go. Flood our souls with your spirit and life. Penetrate and possess our whole being so utterly that our lives may only be a radiance of yours. Shine through us and be so in us that every soul we come in contact with may feel your Presence in our soul. Let them look up and see no longer us, but only Jesus. Stay with us and then we shall begin to shine as you shine, so to shine as to be light to others. The light, O Jesus, will be all from you. None of it will be ours. It will be you shining on others through us. Let us thus praise you in the way you love best by shining on those around us. Let us preach you without preaching, not by words, but by our example; by the catching force — the sympathetic influence of what we do, the evident fullness of the love our hearts bear to you. Amen.[1]

Franklin D. Roosevelt – U.S. President, 20th Century

Almighty God: Our sons, pride of our nation, this day have set upon a mighty endeavor, a struggle to preserve our Republic, our religion, and our civilization, and to set free a suffering humanity.

Lead them straight and true; give strength to their arms, stoutness to their hearts, steadfastness in their faith...fathers, mothers, children, wives, sisters, and brothers of brave men overseas, whose thoughts and prayers are ever with them—help us, Almighty God, to rededicate ourselves in renewed faith in Thee in this hour of great sacrifice.

Many people have urged that I call the nation into a single day of special prayer. But because the road is long and the desire is great, I ask that our people devote themselves in a continuance of prayer. As we rise to each new day, and again when each day is spent, let words of prayer be on our lips, invoking Thy help to our efforts.

Give us strength, too—strength in our daily tasks, to redouble the contributions we make in the physical and the material support of our armed forces.

And let our hearts be stout, to wait out the long travail, to bear sorrows that may come, to impart our courage unto our sons wheresoever they may be.

And, O Lord, give us faith. Give us faith in Thee; faith in our sons; faith in each other; faith in our united crusade.

Let not the keenness of our spirit ever be dulled. Let not the impacts of temporary events, of temporal matters of but fleeting moment—let not these deter us in our unconquerable purpose.

With Thy blessing, we shall prevail over the unholy forces of our enemy. Help us to conquer the apostles of greed and racial arrogances. Lead us to the saving of our country, and with our sister nations into a world unity that will spell a sure peace—a peace invulnerable to the schemings of unworthy men. And a peace that will let all of men live in freedom, reaping the just rewards of their honest toil. Thy will be done, Almighty God. Amen. (June 6, 1944)[2]

Thomas Merton – Catholic theologian, 20th Century

When I am liberated by silence, when I am no longer involved in the measurement of life, but in the living of it, I can discover a form of prayer in which there is effectively no distraction. My whole life becomes a prayer. My whole silence is full of prayer. The world of silence in which I am immersed contributes to my prayer.[3]

George Washington – U.S. President, 18th Century

Whereas it is the duty of all nations to acknowledge the providence of Almighty God, to obey His will, to be grateful for His benefits, and humbly to implore His protection and favor; and Whereas both Houses of Congress have, by their joint committee, requested me "to recommend to the people of the United States a day of public thanksgiving and prayer, to be observed by acknowledging with grateful hearts the many and signal favors of Almighty God, especially by affording them an opportunity peaceably to establish a form of government for their safety and happiness:"

Now, therefore, I do recommend and assign Thursday, the 26th day of November next, to be devoted by the people of these States to the service of that great and glorious Being who is the beneficent author of all the good that was, that is, or that will be; that we may then all unite in rendering unto Him our sincere and humble thanks for His kind care and protection of the people of this country previous to their becoming a nation; for the signal and manifold mercies and the favorable interpositions of His providence in the course and conclusion of the late war....

And also that we may then unite in most humbly offering our prayers and supplications to the great Lord and Ruler of Nations and beseech Him to pardon our national and other transgressions; to enable us all, whether in public or private stations, to perform our several and relative duties properly and punctually; to render our National Government a blessing to all the people by constantly being a Government of wise, just, and constitutional laws, discreetly and faithfully executed and obeyed...to promote the knowledge and practice of true religion and virtue, and the increase of science among them and us; and, generally to grant unto all mankind such a degree of temporal prosperity as He alone knows to be best.[4]

Mary Queen of Scots – Queen of Scotland, 16th Century

Lord my God, I hope in thee; My dear Lord Jesus, set me free; In chains, in pains, I long for thee; On bended knee I adore thee, implore thee To set me free.[5]

Thomas Jefferson – U.S. President, 18th Century

God who gave us life gave us liberty. And can the liberties of a nation be thought secure when we have removed their only firm basis, a conviction in the minds of the people that these liberties are a gift from God? [6]

Queen Elizabeth I – Queen of England, 16th Century

Lorde God Father everlasting, which reigneth over the Kingdoms of men....so teach me, I humbly beseech Thee, thy word, and so strengthen me with thy grace that I may feed thy people with a faithful and a true heart: and rule them prudently with power. Oh Lord, thou hast set me on high, my flesh is frail and weak. If I therefore at any time forget thee, touch my heart, o Lord, that I may again remember thee, if I swell against thee, pluck me down in my own conceit.... I acknowledge, oh my King, without thee my throne is unstable, my seat unsure, my Kingdom tottering, my life uncertain. I see all things in this life subject to mutability, nothing to continue still at one stay.... Create therefore in me, O Lord, a new heart, and so renew my spirit within me that thy law may be my study, thy truth my delight; thy church my care; thy people my crown; thy righteousness my pleasure; thy service my government...so shall this my kingdom through thee be established with peace...[7]

Martin Luther King Jr. – Civil Rights Movement, 20th Century

Well, I don't know what will happen now. We've got some difficult days ahead. But it doesn't matter with me now. Because I've been to the mountaintop. And I don't mind. Like anybody, I would like to live a long life.

Longevity has its place. But I'm not concerned about that now. I just want to do God's will. And He's allowed me to go up to the mountain. And I've looked over. And I've seen the promised land. I may not get there with you. But I want you to know tonight, that we, as a people will get to the promised land. And I'm happy, tonight.

I'm not worried about anything. I'm not fearing any man. Mine eyes have seen the glory of the coming of the Lord (April 3, 1968)[8]

Sir Walter Raleigh – Adventurer, Writer, 16th Century

Give me my scallop-shell of quiet, my staff of faith to walk upon, my scrip of joy, immortal diet, my bottle of salvation, my gown of Glory, hope's true gage; and this I'll take my pilgrimage.[9]

Abraham Lincoln – U.S. President, 19th century

I have been driven many times upon my knees by the overwhelming conviction that I had nowhere else to go. My own wisdom and that of all about me seemed insufficient for that day.[10]

St. Francis of Assisi – Catholic monk, 13th Century

You are holy, Lord, the only God, and Your deeds are wonderful. You are strong. You are great. You are the Most High. You are Almighty. You, Holy Father are King of heaven and earth. You are Three and One, Lord God, all Good. You are Good, all Good, supreme Good, Lord God, living and true. You are love. You are wisdom. You are humility. You are endurance. You are rest. You are peace. You are joy and gladness. You are justice and moderation. You are all our riches, and You suffice for us. You are beauty. You are gentleness. You are our protector. You are our guardian and defender. You are our courage. You are our haven and our hope. You are our faith, our great consolation. You are our eternal life, Great and Wonderful Lord, God Almighty, Merciful Saviour.[11]

Michelangelo - Italian Artist, 16th Century

Lord, make me see thy glory in every place: If mortal beauty sets my heart aglow, Shall not that earthly fire by thine burn low, Extinguisht by the great light of thy grace?

Dear Lord, I cry for thee for help, O raise Me from the misery of this blind woe, Thy spirit alone can save me: let it flow Through will and sense, redeeming what is base.[12]

Beethoven – German Composer, 19th Century

God give me strength to be victorious over myself, for nothing may chain me to this life. O guide my spirit, O raise me from these dark depths, that my soul, transported through Thy wisdom, may fearlessly struggle upward in fiery flight. For Thou alone understandest and canst inspire.[13]

King Robert of France – King of France, 11th Century

O thou almighty Will, Faint are thy children, till Thou come with power; Strength of our good intents, In our frail home, Defence, Calm of Faith's confidence, Come, in this blessed hour!

O thou most tender Love! Deep in our spirits move; Tarry, dear Guest! Quench thou our passion's fire, Raise thou each low desire, Deeds of brave love inspire, Quickener and Rest!

O Light serene and still! Come and our spirit fill, Bring in the day: Guide of our feeble sight Star of our darkest night, Shine on the path of right, Show us the way![14]

Daniel Webster – U.S. Senator and Educator, 19th Century

If we and our posterity reject religious instruction and authority, violate the rules of eternal justice, trifle with the injunctions of morality, and recklessly destroy the political constitution which holds us together, no man can tell how sudden a catastrophe may overwhelm us that shall bury all our glory in profound obscurity.[15]

Endnotes

1 www.worldprayers.org

2 www.historyplace.com/speeches/fdr-prayer.html

3 www.worldprayers.org

4 http://www.night.net/thanksgiving/kwash-11.html

5 Elizabeth Goudge, *A Diary of Prayer* (New York: Coward-McCann, 1966), 231.

6 www.prayforleaders.org/quotes.html

7 Barbara Greene and Victor Gollancz, *God of a Hundred Names* (Garden City, NY: Doubleday and Company, Inc., 1962), 105.

8 www.worldprayers.org

9 Greene and Gollancz, 62.

10 Michael Burlingame, ed., *Lincoln Observed: The Civil War Dispatches of Noah Brooks* (Baltimore, MD: Johns Hopkins University Press, 1998), 210.

11 Greene and Gollancz, 202.

12 www.worldprayers.org

13 Greene and Gollancz, 207.

14 Goudge, 225.

15 Daniel Webster, *The Writings and Speeches of Daniel Webster* (Boston: Little, Brown, & Company, 1903, Vol. XIII, 492. From "The Dignity and Importance of History," February 23, 1852.)

Psalm 116:1-9

The Lord hears us when we call unto Him
I love the Lord, because He hath heard my voice
and my supplications.
Because He hath inclined his ear unto me,
therefore will
I call upon Him as long as I live.
The sorrows of death compassed me, and the pains of
hell gat hold upon me: I found trouble and sorrow.
Then called I upon the name of the Lord; O Lord,
I beseech thee, deliver my soul.
Gracious is the Lord, and righteous; yea,
our God is merciful.
The Lord preserveth the simple:
I was brought low, and He helped me.
Return unto thy rest, O my soul;
for the Lord hath dealt bountifully with thee.
For Thou hast delivered my soul from death, mine
eyes from tears, and my feet from falling.
I will walk before the Lord
in the land of the living.

PATTERNS OF PRAYER

Cleddie Keith

Psalm 121

My help comes from the Lord!!

I will lift up mine eyes unto the hills,
from whence cometh my help.
My help cometh from the Lord,
which made heaven and earth.
He will not suffer thy foot to be moved:
He that keepeth thee will not slumber.
Behold, He that keepeth Israel
shall neither slumber nor sleep.
The Lord is thy keeper:
the Lord is thy shade upon thy right hand.
The sun shall not smite thee by day,
nor the moon by night.
The Lord shall preserve thee from all evil:
He shall preserve thy soul.
The Lord shall preserve thy going out and thy coming
in from this time forth, and even for evermore.

Why Pray by Pattern?

Over the years I have found that patterns of prayer are very beneficial in helping me pray. Scripture makes it clear that from time to time we need to give instruction, or be instructed as to the matter of praying. Patterns help us organize our thoughts. They also help us focus on the Lord.

As a pastor, I have learned how to pray by praying. Talking to God with some guidance always helped me as I learned to commune with the Lord. The following pages are two recommended patterns of prayer which will be helpful to you on your prayer journey: The Ten Commandments and The Lord's Prayer.

PRAYING THE TEN COMMANDMENTS

Exodus 20:3-17

We use this portion of Scripture as a pattern of prayer, because we know that these instructions came straight from the heart of God to maintain order among mankind.

As in any pattern of prayer, you will think of other things to pray for as you use the notes below. Remember that a pattern will always help you in this way. As you pray according to a pattern, the Lord will bring many things to memory that you should remember in prayer. You may even find that you will not be able to pray through an entire pattern at one sitting. That is fine. The goal is to develop a spontaneous and vibrant conversation with the Lord. A pattern only helps you to get started.

FIRST COMMANDMENT

Thou shalt have no other gods before Me.

Today we honor you as the only God; there is none else besides You. We honor You as our Creator. We honor You as sovereign Lord. We worship you as the only God, full of mercy and truth. There is none higher, none more wonderful than You. We praise your wonderful name.

SECOND COMMANDMENT

Thou shalt not make unto thee any graven image...thou shalt not bow down thyself to them, nor serve them: for I the Lord thy God am a jealous God, visiting the iniquity of the fathers upon the children unto the third and fourth generation of them that hate Me.

Anything that stands between you and God is an idol.

We pray blessings and not curses upon our children, blessings to the fourth generation. We also pray blessings on our nation, our leaders and our communities. We trust God for the best possible He has for them.

Lord, help us to notice when something seems to be more important than You; when something comes between us and Your love and plan for us.

THIRD COMMANDMENT

Thou shalt not take the name of the Lord thy God in vain; for the Lord will not hold him guiltless that taketh His name in vain.

God, You reveal Yourself to me through Your name. The Bible gives you several names. They all help me to understand who You really are and how much You really love me.

YOU ARE THE LORD:

Jehovah-Tsidkenu — God is our Righteousness (Jeremiah 23:5)
Jehovah-M'Kaddesh — God Sanctifies me (Psalm 23:5)
Jehovah-Shalom — God is my Peace (Psalm 23:2)
Jehovah-Shammah — God is Present (Ezekiel 48:35)
Jehovah-Rophe — God is my Healer (Psalm 30:2)
Jehovah-Jireh — God is my Provider (Genesis 22:14)
Jehovah-Nissi — God is my Standard-Bearer (Exodus 17:15)
Jehovah-Rohi — God is my Shepherd (Psalm 23:1)

FOURTH COMMANDMENT

Remember the sabbath day, to keep it holy.

God Himself is my Sabbath or rest; and there remains a rest for the people of God (see Heb. 4:9-10). I trust You to do what I cannot do. I want You, Lord. I rest in Your love, in Your provision. I refuse to be fearful. I refuse to panic. I rest in Your love for me.

FIFTH COMMANDMENT

Honor thy father and thy mother: that thy days may be long upon the land which the Lord thy God giveth thee.

We pray concerning the rebellion in the hearts of youth. Lord, I pray for the children, all children. Lord, please turn the hearts of the children back to the fathers, back toward their families. Please mend the brokenness among families and help our children to have a heartfelt love and respect for their parents. (See Malachi 4:6.)

We pray for parents, that their hearts would turn to their children; to love them, to raise them with honor and in the fear of the Lord.

SIXTH COMMANDMENT

Thou shalt not kill.

We pray for a respect for life across America. We take it as a personal assault on our faith when someone is murdered. We pray for domestic tranquility and harmony in the homes.

Lord, no one hates murder more than You do. I pray for Your Presence in our cities and towns. But I also pray for Your Presence in our hearts so that the spirits of murder and death will have no place to rest. Let healing come to our hearts and to our land.

SEVENTH COMMANDMENT

Thou shalt not commit adultery.

Oh Lord, I take authority over the spirit of lust that drives men and women to compromise their lives. We pray that the marriage beds will be undefiled and that men and women will look upon one another as temples of the Holy Spirit. I pray for holiness to be born in the hearts of all Your people. I pray that Your love will overcome the lust that so many fight and hate. May we see our spouses as the wonderful gifts from the Lord that they really are. Teach us to love them with everything that is in us.

EIGHTH COMMANDMENT

Thou shalt not steal.

I pray that men will not steal but work with their hands. We pray that men will give an honest day's work for an honest day's pay. Lord, help me not to be greedy and envious of others. You take wonderful care of me. Besides, if I need anything, all I have to do is ask You. You are my provider. I love You. Thank You, Lord.

NINTH COMMANDMENT

Thou shalt not bear false witness against thy neighbour.

I pray that men will not become false witnesses against their neighbors. I pray that our reputations will be safe in the hands of others and visa versa. Help us to be truthful to ourselves and to You, Lord. You can only forgive us if we are honest with ourselves and with You. May truth grow up from the deepest part of our hearts. May I learn to love the truth and cherish it.

TENTH COMMANDMENT

Thou shalt not covet thy neighbor's house...nor any thing that is thy neighbor's.

I pray that men will find themselves content no matter what their situation. Help me to be content. Help me to rejoice with another's promotion or new car or whatever you bless them with. You give me everything I need. I am happy for Your provision. Thank You, Lord. I love You!

PRAYING THE LORD'S PRAYER

Matthew 6:9-13

When Jesus' disciples asked Him how to pray, He gave them a pattern of prayer, commonly referred to as the Lord's Prayer.

I remember my father buying a sewing machine for my mother. He thought he had really done something. He had—he had bought himself a new toy! My mom never used it, but my father became a pretty good tailor. He could make dresses and shirts or whatever he wanted to make. For the most part it was just a piece of furniture that brought us a lot of laughs over the years. He would buy a pattern for a dress and then he would improvise. My father was very creative. He could build a beautiful horse trailer in the front driveway of our home. The pattern was in his head. It amazed me. The same is true for prayer. When you have a pattern, you make beautiful things happen.

As you pray the Lord's Prayer, remember it is our Father you are talking to. He is not off making worlds somewhere. He is not too busy for you. He is closer to us than our next breath. Praise Him for all His wonderful works. Prayer is like dancing. C.S. Lewis said, "As long as you are watching your feet you are not dancing—you are only learning to dance."

For several years I have prayed the Lord's Prayer in a systematic fashion. I have found this to be a pattern of prayer that my very creative heavenly Father can form into wonderful, surprising, and beautiful responses.

Let us pray: Our Father,

I praise you, God that you are my loving Father. You are more than my creator—You are Dad. You are the One and only protector of my soul. I love You, Father. I worship You.

which art in heaven,

Isaiah 55:9 says the heavens are above the earth, and so are God's ways higher than ours. Lord, I seek guidance from Heaven's perspective. Jesus set the example by doing only what He saw His Father doing. I, too, know not what to do without Your loving Presence leading me. I cannot do this myself. I need the help that only comes from Heaven.

Hallowed be Thy name.

You have revealed Yourself to us through Your name. I call upon You by the names through which You have revealed Yourself to mankind.

Lord, You are everything I need and want. By Your name, all the demons on earth and in hell tremble. By Your name, nature comes under Your Lordship and people are healed. But most wonderfully, by Your name, average people like me can come to know You as Savior and Lord. Thank You, Lord, in Jesus' name, for forgiving me and loving me.

Thy Kingdom come. Thy will be done....

This is not a passive prayer! To pray this prayer means to stomp my foot and mean business. Every person has a will to surrender — for God to have His will, I have to surrender my will. To yield my will is to humble myself. I can be humiliated by others, but only I can humble myself (see James 4:10).

Give us this day our daily bread...

Jesus you said Your source of food was to do the will of Your Father (see John 4:34). What satisfies me is to know that I satisfy Your purpose. You are my necessary bread (see John 6:35). You are the bread of Heaven, and You also want me to look to You for my daily natural provision.

Forgive us our debts, as we forgive our debtors....

It is necessary to forgive if I expect to be heard when I pray, so Lord, I choose to forgive. (See Matthew 18:21-35.)

Lead us not into temptation, but deliver us from evil....

Jesus, you were driven into the wilderness of temptation. It was there that the enemy attempted to cause You to forget who You are, saying: "If [you are] the Son of God..." (Luke. 4:3). If the enemy can get me to forget who I am, he can get me to do whatever he wants me to do. Who am I? I will declare who I am in Christ. (See Galatians 3:26; Romans 8:37; Revelation 1:6.)

Ephesians 4:27 says not to "give place" to the devil. This means do not give the enemy a legal right to be in my life. Areas where the enemy can enter are things like fear, hate, witchcraft, or sexual immorality.

For Thine is the Kingdom, and the power, and the glory....

Psalm 108:5 says that Your glory is over all the earth. The glory of God is over my family, my friends, my loved ones, those with whom I worship. I pray that You will spread His wings over them and protect them.

FOUR LEVELS OF PRAYER

In addition to a variety of scriptural patterns of prayer, there are also a variety of levels of prayer. Here are four such levels: crisis praying, petitional praying, relational praying, and intercession.

CRISIS PRAYING

Crisis praying is one of the most emotional levels of prayer. We realize that things are out of control and demand a miracle. At this point we do not stop to think that this is the prerequisite for miracles: things must be out of control. Jesus spoke to this issue in the story of Peter walking with Him on the water. (See Matthew 14:26-32.) Peter had taken his eyes off Jesus. When he saw his predicament and was beginning to sink, Peter cried out to the Lord, "Help me!"

That is a prayer that most of us have prayed at one time or another. Jesus, ever the Teacher, used the circumstance to teach Peter a valuable lesson. He reached out and saved Peter from the powerful waves, saying, "Why did you doubt?" The word *doubt* means to be pulled in two different directions. In times of crisis we may feel like we are being pulled apart.

It is a crisis when your automobile is hydroplaning down the highway at 60 miles an hour. That is not the time for a long pretentious prayer. The law of aerodynamics has taken over, and things are out of your control.

"Jesus! Help!" is usually the order of the moment. This is what is meant by crisis praying.

PETITIONAL PRAYING

Petitional praying may be considered "to make a formal request," because the term is used in law and government concerning legal issues. The story of Esther is a story of petition. She knew the protocol of human government full well, and was valiant in her petition of the king. When she went into the presence of the king uninvited, she knew that her life was at risk; but she had a confidence that she had been born into the kingdom for such a moment. She made her petition at all costs by stating, "If I perish, I perish" (Esther 4:16). People who know their destiny are not afraid of taking risks. To petition in this case is to ask or to request.

First John 5:14-15 is an example of petitional prayer. It reads, "And this is the confidence that we have in Him, that, if we ask any thing according to His will, He heareth us: and if we know that He hear us, whatsoever we ask, we know that we have the petitions that we desired of Him."

RELATIONAL PRAYING

Relational prayers are just what they imply. There is a relationship that exists between persons. Good relationships equal good communications. When my father died at an early age, my sister Karissa was only seven years old; his death shattered her world. My mother loved the Word of God. She knew it well and she knew Him well. I remember how she comforted my sister in those difficult days. I can still hear her say, "Fear not, little flock; for it is your Father's good pleasure to give you the kingdom" (Luke. 12:32). My mother was laying down the true foundation for prayer in my sister's life.

Relational praying is talking to God as someone you have a relationship with, someone who loves you and has your best interest at heart. It is our privilege to come to Him as "Our Father." It is in this relationship that we can claim His promises, pardon, forgiveness, and grace, we can claim our daily bread; and we can claim a stingless death, and ultimately resurrection and an everlasting life.

INTERCESSORY PRAYER

To distinguish intercessory prayer from other types of prayer it is necessary to define what is meant by the term intercessor. Intercessors are persons who stand between—they are mediators. A more familiar term would be a lawyer.

Several years ago, I had to call on an attorney to take care of a legal situation for me. One day several weeks later, he called to say the matter was finished. I told him that I had learned something very valuable from him. He was curious as to how God had used him to teach me something. I told him that Jesus is revealed in the Scripture as the Advocate, and for a man to become a Christian, he must totally turn his case over to Him. There was silence on the phone that day and then I asked, " Friend, have you turned your case over to Him?"

Jesus is our chief example of what an intercessor really should be. He lives to make intercession for us. The Holy Spirit is ever pleading our case to Jesus and Jesus is ever pleading our case to the Father. (See Hebrews 7:25; Romans 8:27.)

My father-in-law, Hardie Weathers, was a notorious intercessor and he taught me the importance of prayer. He reminded me of what David said in Psalms 109:4: "I am...prayer." Hardie would go to prayer just like a man would go to work on a secular job. He would break for lunch and then go back to the important ministry of prayer. I can still hear him say, "We learn to walk by walking, we learn to run by running, we learn to talk by talking, we learn to sing by singing, we learn to give by giving, and we learn to pray by praying."

DISCOVERING THE POWER OF PRAYER

God wants to answer our prayers. He has proven that to me time and time again over the years. There is nothing He will not do for those who call to Him in sincerity and humility. I have seen broken marriages healed. I have watched as children angrily and tragically left their homes, only to return later in repentance and fresh love for their parents. I have seen people healed from the most terrible diseases and I have seen hope restored to alcoholics and drug addicts. I have seen all this through the power of prayer—prayer that the Lord taught me as I prayed.

He will do the same for you. Take time to pray. Your heavenly Father loves you! He is waiting for you right now. Find a quiet place, close your eyes, think of your Father in Heaven and begin talking to Him as you would talk to your best friend. After all, you may not realize it yet, but He is your best friend.

SECTION FOUR

LORD, HOW SHOULD WE PRAY?

PRAYERS TO HELP YOU TALK TO GOD

Dian Layton

Matthew 6:9-12

The Lord's Prayer

Our Father
which art in heaven,
Hallowed be thy name.
Thy kingdom come.
Thy will be done in earth,
as it is in heaven.
Give us this day
our daily bread.
And forgive us our debts,
as we forgive our debtors.
And lead us not into temptation,
but deliver us from evil:
For thine is the kingdom,
and the power,
and the glory, for ever.
Amen.

God Wants Us to Pray

God is waiting to hear you pray. Prayer is simply talking to God. The best prayers are the ones we say using our own words. The best prayers also are prayers that are not one-sided conversations. God wants to speak to you.

Learning to hear God's voice is an exciting adventure. His voice will come to you in many ways. He may come to you more as a feeling inside, like a nudging or an impression. You might see a picture in your mind, or you may suddenly have an idea that you know you didn't think up yourself.

In this section, we have provided a variety of prayers that are powerful and effective. This is just a starting place. As soon as you pray these prayers, many wonderful ideas and important things to pray for will come to your mind.

So, find a quiet place, get a pen and notebook, and be ready for conversation with the Living God.

Prayer for Government Leaders —

When the righteous are in authority, the people rejoice... (Proverbs 29:2).

Lord, You have the ultimate authority; You *are* the ultimate authority. You are high above all principality, and power, and might, and dominion, and every name that is named not only in this world, but also in that which is to come.

I pray for the leaders of our country. They need Your help, Lord! You've said in Your Word that if anyone lacks wisdom, all they need to do is ask; and You said there is safety in a multitude of counselors. So, I pray that every person in any position of authority will be led by Your Spirit. Give them wise counsel and wise counselors. Give them divine guidance. Help them to understand the times we are living in and show them the right course to take.

Put a hedge of protection around every leader and their family. Bless them, Lord! Bless them with peace, prosperity and an inner confidence that You are in control. Amen.

I exhort therefore, that, first of all, supplications, prayers, intercessions, and giving of thanks, be made for all men; for kings, and for all that are in authority; that we may lead a quiet and peaceable life in all godliness and honesty (1 Timothy 2:1-2).

See also 1 Chronicles 12:32, Isaiah 58:2, Ephesians 1:21, James 1:5; 3:17, Proverbs 11:14.

PRAYER FOR THE MILITARY —

I will call on the Lord, who is worthy to be praised: so shall I be saved from mine enemies (2 Samuel 22:4).

Neither know we what to do: but our eyes are upon Thee (2 Chronicles 20:12).

Save us from our enemies, Lord! Turn back the forces that attack us, and rescue us from every evil intention.

Lord, we pray for all military personnel. Thank you for the men and women who have stepped forward and reported for duty. Give them confidence, not in their own abilities, but in the fact that You are with them. Help them to realize how righteous the cause for battle really is. Give them courage and strength. In times when they are not sure what to do, may they turn their eyes and look to You for help. And may their families take comfort in Your Word....

Fear thou not; for I am with thee: be not dismayed; for I am thy God: I will strengthen thee; yea, I will help thee; yea, I will uphold thee with the right hand of My righteousness. Behold, all they that were incensed against thee shall be ashamed and confounded: they shall be as nothing; and they that strive with thee shall perish. Thou shalt seek them, and shalt not find them, even them that contended with thee: they that war against thee shall be as nothing, and as a thing of nought. For I the Lord thy God will hold thy right hand, saying unto thee, Fear not; I will help thee (Isaiah 41:10-13).

PRAYER FOR SCHOOLS—

And the spirit of the Lord shall rest upon him, the spirit of wisdom and understanding, the spirit of counsel and might, the spirit of knowledge and of the fear of the Lord; And shall make him of quick understanding in the fear of the Lord: and he shall not judge after the sight of his eyes, neither reprove after the hearing of his ears (Isaiah 11:2-3).

Father God, I pray for our schools. Pour out Your Spirit and fill the children and young people of this nation with light that penetrates their darkness.

I pray for Your protection and safety for each child, teacher, and administrator. Help us to keep praying for Your divine protection not only during these difficult days but also after these times pass by.

I pray for every Christian student and every Christian teacher. Give them strength to proclaim the truth in the midst of a so-called secular society that is filled with people longing to know You. Help them realize they are ambassadors for the King of kings. Give them a sense of destiny and purpose. As citizens of Heaven, they are representing You here on earth. Give them divine protection and holy boldness to declare You in every classroom, every office, every hallway, and every playground across America.

You told us to pray, "Let Your kingdom come," and that is what we pray for the schools of America. Let Your kingdom come and let Your will be done! Be high and lifted up across this land and draw thousands and thousands of young people to You. Amen!

Now then we are ambassadors for Christ, as though God did beseech you by us: we pray you in Christ's stead, be ye reconciled to God (2 Corinthians 5:20).

And I, if I be lifted up from the earth, will draw all men unto Me (John 12:32).

Whom shall He teach knowledge? and whom shall He make to understand doctrine? them that are weaned from the milk, and drawn from the breasts. For precept must be upon precept, precept upon precept; line upon line, line upon line; here a little, and there a little (Isaiah 28:9-10).

And all thy children shall be taught of the Lord; and great shall be the peace of thy children (Isaiah 54:13).

The eyes of your understanding being enlightened; that ye may know what is the hope of His calling, and what the riches of the glory of His inheritance in the saints, and what is the exceeding greatness of His power to us-ward who believe, according to the working of His mighty power (Ephesians 1:18-19).

PRAYER FOR THE CHILDREN —

And all thy children shall be taught of the Lord; and great shall be the peace of thy children (Isaiah 54:13).

Jesus, You never change. You are the same yesterday, today, and forever. When You walked on this earth, You took young children in Your arms, put Your hands upon them, and blessed them.

Now we're asking You to touch our children. Take them in Your arms, put Your hands on them, and bless them, Lord! Fill their hearts with peace, and fill them with Your Holy Spirit. Fill them with joy and love, and with the confidence and power to do what is right.

Bless them, protect them, and keep Your hand upon their lives. Lord, we cannot be with them every minute of the day, but You can be with them and You are with them. Send Your angels to watch our children and to keep them safe.

And Lord, not only do we ask for Your protection, we also ask You to use our children. Your Word says that from the mouths of children comes praise so powerful that it silences the enemy. Well, the voice of the enemy has been much too loud in this generation! May the voices of children across this nation be lifted up with praise so powerful that it silences the enemy! May this generation of children be a generation who know You, Lord. Amen.

Jesus Christ the same yesterday, and to day, and for ever (Hebrews 13:8).

Jesus said, Suffer little children, and forbid them not, to come unto Me: for of such is the kingdom of heaven. And He laid His hands on them (Matthew 19:14-15a).

Take heed that ye despise not one of these little ones; for I say unto you, That in heaven their angels do always behold the face of My Father which is in heaven (Matthew 18:10).

Out of the mouth of babes and [young children] hast Thou ordained strength because of Thine enemies, that Thou mightest still the enemy and the avenger (Psalm 8:2).

And it shall come to pass afterward, that I will pour out My Spirit upon all flesh; and your sons and your daughters shall prophesy, your old men shall dream dreams, your young men shall see visions. (Joel 2:28; see also Acts 2:17).

Arise, cry out in the night...pour out thine heart like water before the face of the Lord: lift up thy hands toward Him for the life of thy young children (Lamentations 2:19).

PRAYER FOR FAMILIES —

He shall feed His flock like a shepherd: He shall gather the lambs with His arm, and carry them in His bosom, and shall gently lead those that are with young (Isaiah 40:11).

The families of America need You, Lord! In a world of brokenness and division, we pray according to the last verse of the Old Testament: "Turn the heart of the fathers to the children, and the heart of the children to their fathers" (Malachi. 4:6a).

God, we ask You to turn the hearts of parents and children toward each other and toward You. In a world of confusion and uncertainty, our homes can be places of security and rest if You are there, Lord Jesus. When You are the central Person in our homes, You will give us inner confidence, no matter what is going on outside.

We pray that fathers and mothers will be the pastors of their homes. As they shepherd their little flock — Jesus, be their Shepherd, also. Gently lead parents. Give them wisdom in raising their children. Give them patience. And give them an extraordinary ability to see beyond the daily routines of life into the future.

Help parents realize that the days of childhood are precious days of planting seeds. The lives of their children are tender fields. Help parents to plant carefully and with purpose so that their children will have all they need to become all that You have intended for them.

You do have intentions for our children and for our families. You have dreams and plans for our futures that are very, very good. You are knocking on the door of each home, and on every heart. Help us to say, "Come in, Lord Jesus! Come in and be King and Shepherd and Savior of our lives. Amen."

Behold, I stand at the door, and knock: if any man hear My voice, and open the door, I will come in to him, and will sup with him, and he with Me (Revelation 3:20).

And He shall turn the heart of the fathers to the children, and the heart of the children to their fathers, lest I come and smite the earth with a curse (Malachi 4:6).

And I will give you pastors according to mine heart, which shall feed you with knowledge and understanding (Pastor your family) (Jeremiah 3:15).

For I know the thoughts that I think toward you, saith the Lord, thoughts of peace, and not of evil, to give you an expected end (Jeremiah 29:11).

And ye shall teach them your children, speaking of them when thou sittest in thine house, and when thou walkest by the way, when thou liest down, and when thou risest up. And thou shalt write them upon the door posts of thine house, and upon thy gates: that your days may be multiplied, and the days of your children, in the land which the Lord sware unto your fathers to give them, as the days of heaven upon the earth (Deuteronomy 11:19-21).

Prayer for Comfort —

He healeth the broken in heart, and bindeth up their wounds (Psalms 147:3).

Jesus, You said, "Blessed are they that mourn: for they shall be comforted." I'm claiming that promise today, Lord, because I really, really need to be comforted.

You said that Your Holy Spirit is "the Comforter." Well, here I am, Holy Spirit, asking You to comfort me. Wrap me up in the soft blanket of Your presence. Cover me and hide me and heal my heart.

Your Word gives me comfort and hope. So, right now, I want to pray Psalm 23 in my own words, as if it were written just to me...

Lord, You are my shepherd; I will not lack any good thing.
You let me rest in green pastures: You lead me beside clear, peaceful streams.
You restore and renew the very essence of who I am.
You guide me in the right way and I pray that I will bring honor to Your name.
Even when I walk through the valley of the shadow of death, I will not be afraid:
Because You are with me; Your guidance and protection comfort me.
You set a banquet before me — right in the middle

of trouble!
You anoint me and fill me to overflowing with
Your Holy Spirit.
I am confident that goodness and mercy will be
with me all the days of my life:
And I will live in Your Presence forever.
Amen.

For whatsoever things were written aforetime were written for our learning, that we through patience and comfort of the scriptures might have hope (Romans 15:4).

But the Comforter, which is the Holy Ghost, whom the Father will send in My name, He shall teach you all things, and bring all things to your remembrance, whatsoever I have said unto you. Peace I leave with you, my peace I give unto you: not as the world giveth, give I unto you. Let not your heart be troubled, neither let it be afraid (John 14:26-27).

Blessed are they that mourn: for they shall be comforted (Matthew 5:4).

PRAYER FOR COURAGE —

I would have fainted, unless I had believed to see the goodness of the Lord in the land of the living. Wait on the Lord: be of good courage, and He shall strengthen thine heart: wait, I say, on the Lord (Psalm 27:13-14).

Give me courage, Lord. Give me the ability to keep going and to never give up. Help me realize that You really are God and that You really do control all things. I believe that I will yet see Your goodness in this land, in my family, and in my heart. You will complete what You have begun. You will not give up.

Give me courage, Lord. Give me the ability to see beyond my circumstances. Help me to lift my eyes higher and look at what I cannot see. By an act of my will, I choose to look at You. You made Heaven and earth. Your Word says that You call every star by name and that You hold everything in place by the Word of Your power. In all that greatness, You have also promised never to leave or forsake me.

With You on my side, what do I have to fear? With You on my side, who can be against me?! The choice before me is simple. I choose to trust in You with all my heart. I choose to be very courageous, knowing that God will give strength to my heart. Amen!

See also Psalm 121:1-2, Psalm 147:4, Philippians 1:6, 2 Corinthians 4:18, Colossians 1:16, Romans 8:31

PRAYER FOR HELP —

Let us therefore come boldly to the throne of grace, that we may obtain mercy, and find grace to help in time of need (Hebrews 4:16).

God is our refuge and strength, a very present help in trouble (Psalm 46:1).

Lord, I need help. In the past, when I needed help, I ran to the refrigerator. Sometimes I ran to the shopping mall. Sometimes I ran to the television set, trying to hide my desperate need behind a world of fantasy; or I climbed back into bed, hoping sleep would provide an escape.

Not so today. Today I run to You. I run to You and cry out in my time of need. I pour out my trouble and my complaint. I ask You to somehow intervene in my circumstances before they completely overcome me. I need a miracle. Show me what to do! Provide a way for things to work out; make a way where there seems to be absolutely no way.

Help me, Lord! Amen.

Trust in Him at all times; ye people, pour out your heart before Him: God is a refuge for us (Psalm 62:8).

For I the Lord thy God will hold thy right hand, saying unto thee, Fear not; I will help thee (Isaiah 41:13).

See also Psalm 102:1, 121:1-2, 124:7-8

PRAYER FOR STRENGTH —

And He said unto me, My grace is sufficient for thee: for my strength is made perfect in weakness. Most gladly therefore will I rather glory in my weaknesses, that the power of Christ may rest upon me. Therefore I take pleasure in weakness, in reproaches, in necessities, in persecutions, in distresses for Christ's sake: for when I am weak, then am I strong. (See 2 Corinthians 12:9-10.)

Lord, I'm so tired. I just can't do this anymore…

When I say those words, I can hear Your response: That's right. You can't. Now…will you let Me?

I guess that's exactly what You meant when You said, "My strength is made perfect in weakness." I really won't experience Your strength until I reach the end of my own.

Well, I've reached that end, Lord. I'm worn out and tired. My heart is so overwhelmed that I can't even find my way to You…so please lead me. Lead me into Your Presence, and wash away my weariness.

I stand here before You, and I lift my hands. I need You, Jesus. I cannot go another step until You strengthen me. Here, from the end of the earth, I cry out to You! Strengthen my heart! Strengthen my body! Strengthen my mind! Strengthen my love for You! Amen.

See also Psalm 31:24, 61:2, Isaiah 40:29, 31

PRAYER FOR WISDOM —

...that ye might be filled with the knowledge of His will in all wisdom and spiritual understanding (Colossians 1:9).

If any of you lack wisdom, let him ask of God, that giveth to all men liberally, and upbraideth not; and it shall be given him (James 1:5).

Lord, You are Wisdom. You know absolutely everything. You know the beginning and the end. You know the thoughts of every person, and You know what the future will bring. You created us to live each day, walking and talking with You, but sadly, we most often choose to struggle through our lives without You.

I don't want to live like that. I want You to be intensely involved with my daily life. I want to hear Your voice saying, "This is the way...go here, or go there...do this, or do that..." Teach me to hear Your voice. Teach me to recognize the many ways You communicate with me; and help me to respond quickly to Your direction.

Life lived in constant communication with the Creator of the universe—that is how I will have wisdom. I want to begin today. Right now, I surrender control of every decision and every plan to You, Lord Jesus. I choose not to trust my own understanding, but to trust You. Amen.

See also Psalm 32:8, Proverbs 2:3-6, 3:5-7, Isaiah 30:21

Prayer for Peace —

And the earth was without form, and void; and darkness was upon the face of the deep. And the Spirit of God moved upon the face of the waters. And God said, Let there be light: and there was light (Genesis 1:2-3).

Lord, I know that at Creation, the world was a chaotic mass. That is exactly the way my world seems sometimes: unorganized, empty, and really, really dark. Lord, I need You to speak to my world! I need You to say, "Let there be Light!" You spoke to Your disciples in the boat, when they were in a huge storm. Their world was certainly looking dark and chaotic...and there, in the middle of their distress, they called out to You. You stood up and spoke directly to the storm: "Peace. Be still." And the winds and the waves went calm.

So right now, I cry out to You in my distress. I pour out my trouble and my complaint and my fears...and right now, I hear You speaking those same words to me: "Peace. Be still." I see Your hand stretched toward my circumstances, and I see the winds and waves growing calm. Thank You for Your peace. Thank You for answering me in times of trouble. And thank You for always being with me. Amen.

And He arose, and rebuked the wind, and said unto the sea, Peace, be still. And the wind ceased, and there was a great calm (Mark 4:39).

See also Psalm 18:6, 142:2, John 14:27, Philippians 4:7

GETTING TO KNOW GOD

[God] Hath in these last days spoken unto us by His Son, whom He hath appointed heir of all things, by whom also He made the worlds; who being the brightness of His glory, and the express image of His person, and upholding all things by the word of His power, when He had by Himself purged our sins, sat down on the right hand of the Majesty on high (Hebrews 1:2-3).

God really, really loves you. Yes, you! This book is about prayer. Praying is communication with God, and it's not one-sided conversation. God wants to reveal His love for us; He wants to speak to us. And when God talks, He doesn't just use words. He also uses pictures, visions, ideas, dreams, melodies, symbolic actions....

God spoke to us in the form of His Son, Jesus Christ. He was the greatest message the world has ever received. He was a message from the Creator of the universe, saying, "I love you."

God loves you so much that He took upon Himself the form of mere mortal men, and humbled Himself—not only to walk on this earth in human flesh, but also to die. Have you heard His message? Have you responded?

Here is a simple prayer that you can pray...

God, I want to know You. I have heard about You. I have prayed to You. But I have never really entered into the kind of relationship where You speak to me and I recognize Your voice.

You revealed Yourself to this world as the Man Christ Jesus. I believe that. I believe that Jesus walked on this earth. I believe He died on the cross. And, I believe it was a personal message…to me. I want to say yes to Your invitation of friendship. I want to live each day in a relationship with You. And I have a feeling deep inside that my life is actually just beginning….

I am come that they might have life, and that they might have it more abundantly (John 10:10b).

…made Himself of no reputation, and took upon Him the form of a servant, and was made in the likeness of men: and being found in fashion as a man, He humbled Himself, and became obedient unto death, even the death of the cross (Philippians 2:7-8).

And this is life eternal, that they might know Thee the only true God, and Jesus Christ, whom Thou hast sent (John 17:3).

AFTER YOU PRAY

During your prayer time, many other thoughts will come to mind. Those thoughts are prayer concerns of your heart. Take a few minutes to write them down and then begin to pray for them in your own words.

The more we talk to God, the more He wants to talk to us. After you have prayed, take a few minutes to listen quietly. You may be surprised by what you hear the Lord saying to you. His words always comfort and encourage us. They always draw us closer to Him.

Think of some people who need you to pray each prayer for them. List them by name.

Please use the journal pages we provided for you at the back of the book.

FROM THE FATHER'S HEART TO YOURS

Charles Slagle

Psalm 125

The wicked shall not rule over thee!

They that trust in the Lord shall be as mount Zion,
which cannot be removed, but abideth for ever.
As the mountains are round about Jerusalem,
so the Lord is round about His people
from henceforth even for ever.
For the rod of the wicked shall not
rest upon the lot of the righteous;
lest the righteous put forth their hands
unto iniquity.
Do good, O Lord, unto those that be good,
and to them that are upright in their hearts.
As for such as turn aside unto their crooked ways,
the Lord shall lead them forth with the workers of
iniquity: but peace shall be upon Israel.

From the Father's Heart to Yours

Did you know that God wants to talk to you as much as you want to talk to Him? In fact, the Lord has much to say to us if we only knew to quiet our souls and listen. Most of us always thought that prayer was a monologue. But that is not what prayer is at all. Prayer is dialogue between us and God. Life would be pretty boring if our conversations with friends were all one-sided. In fact, we would not have many friends at all if that were the way we communicated. True friendship, true love, true companionship, and trust are nurtured in the exchange of feelings and desires. The same is true with your Lord, who has much to tell you.

In this very special section, you will find prayers that are the heart cries of many, many people today. But there is something special here. These prayers have answers from the heart of our loving heavenly Father, who wants to comfort us, teach us, and draw us close to His heart. You will be surprised at how He responds to these prayers.

These prayers were offered to the Lord by Charles Slagle. The responses came to him as he waited quietly before the Lord.

WHY, WHY, WHY?

PRAYER:

Why, why, why? Lord, my mind is tortured with why-questions. If You really love us, why would You let such pain come into our lives? You allow violence and cruelty to stalk the earth. How can I believe in You or trust You? I want to, but how can I?

RESPONSE FROM THE LORD:

My frustrated friend,

Yes, nothing makes sense right now. I know your doubts; I feel your anguish, while I remind you that in this present world I cannot guarantee you or anyone else a life devoid of pain. When I visited this world in the Person of My Son Jesus Christ, even I could not avoid it.

I know this seems incredible to you at this moment, but has it occurred to you that I still experience pain? Yes, as long as any person hurts, I hurt also. I do not live unscathed from the agonies that befall My human offspring, or the pains of any of My creatures, for that matter. But there is a plan. It is a far greater plan than your finite mind can perceive, treasured one. I AM fulfilling that plan for the good of all—yes, for the infinite joy of all—and what is happening now is a necessary part of its fulfillment.

You must find your hope and reason for being in Me alone; these cannot be found in what occurs or does not occur in your earthly environment. You already have seen the futility of trying to figure things out. I alone possess all power. Only I can remedy all problems. Only I can cause all things to be well. I assure you that all will be well, and that there is more at stake than these temporal events, which for now seem so baffling to you.

Yours with Deepest Tenderness,
Father

ARE YOU JUDGING US??

PRAYER:

God, are you judging us? Why would You pour out harsh judgment on us instead of showing up to heal our world and help us to learn Your ways?

RESPONSE FROM THE LORD:

Dear Child,

No, I AM not judging anyone in the sense that religious minds often term as judgment. I was in the world two thousand years ago in a special way when I came in the heart of My Son, Jesus Christ. And I did not come to accuse and condemn the world. I came to set people free from sin and death, not to imprison them in their pain. I was in the world, reconciling all of its peoples to Myself, and I have not changed My policy, nor has My personality undergone any alteration.

At this stage of your journey, there is no way that you can understand the honor and the joy I have in store for humankind. The time is coming when I will show up in the world, and even now it is being prepared for My arrival. Meanwhile, be still and know that I AM God. The nations are in My good hands, and the day will come when all the earth will rejoice in My unfailing love.

Yours with All Power Always,
Your Loving Father

IN TIMES OF CONFUSION

PRAYER:

From all of the reports, it looks like terribly hard times are coming, and I feel lost in a cloud of darkness. Lord, I want so much to be a blessing in this world, but right now I feel so helpless, so useless.

RESPONSE FROM THE LORD:

Struggling Conqueror,

You must test all things and hold fast to that which is good. Do the thoughts bombarding your mind at this moment enhance your hope in Me? Or do they foster unceasing analysis, confusion, and worry? My highest priority is that you live constantly in the mind of Christ— His mentality, His servant-hearted love, His childlike faith, His unshakable serenity.

Your Lord once commanded a storm to cease that rose on the Sea of Galilee. The winds were real, the waves were real, the threat was real. It was a true storm. It just was not as true as I AM! Your Savior knew that. That is why He could sleep in the back of a small boat that rose and plunged amidst watery wave mountains while His cherished disciples were frantic. Decide now to abide in His peace that defies reason and transcends understanding.

I appreciate your trust.
Yours with All Power, Forever!
Dad

LORD, ARE YOU REALLY IN CONTROL?

PRAYER:

Oh Lord, please help me. I look grownup, but inside I'm just a scared little kid. I can't concentrate on my work. I feel guilty for feeling bad, I feel guilty for feeling good. I feel guilty for laughing, I feel guilty for crying. I feel hollow inside. Nothing makes any sense. What kind of future can I expect for my little ones? What lies ahead for all of the world's children? God, please — will You tell me what is happening? Are You really in control of this miserable planet?

RESPONSE FROM THE LORD:

Weeping and Bewildered One,

Oh yes, I AM in control. And believe it or not, I AM in loving control. My heart aches for your pain. Yet My heart also rejoices because I see what lies ahead, although your mortal eyes cannot see it. Our kingdom of love is coming! Love will reign.

Are you aware that I raised up your homeland to be a safe haven for the world's weary, to be a towering beacon of hope for all who weep under the shadow of despair? Yes, but because greed and lust for power have captured the hearts of many of My children, the light of this nation has been waning for decades. Even so! When My present work in the earth is done, your light will shine more brilliantly than ever! And better yet, yours will be but one among many splendid national lights, for the time is soon coming when the whole earth will blaze with the light of My glory! The light of Love will permeate all.

Child, never fear. Those who have perpetuated violence and abuse will meet with justice. Sterling Justice. Yet, the reality is, I AM not punishing anyone. I AM letting people — worldwide — arrive at the end of themselves so they will yearn for Me. You are not wrong to suppose that more sorrows await this world. But refuse to fear, and cast every care upon Me. Focus on the plan and not on the pain. There is more to life than this earthly existence. Your children are in My tender keeping. Your future is bright and secure. Christ defeated death and swallowed it up in life, and you are more than a conqueror because He dwells in you. He is the healing Light of the world.

Yours with Deepest Compassion,
Father

POWER OF A PRAYING NATION

Don Nori

Psalm 130

There is always forgiveness with Thee,
O Lord!!
Out of the depths have I cried unto Thee,
O Lord.
Lord, hear my voice:
let Thine ears be attentive
to the voice of my supplications.
If Thou, Lord, shouldest mark iniquities,
O Lord, who shall stand?
But there is forgiveness with Thee,
that Thou mayest be feared.
I wait for the Lord, my soul doth wait,
and in His word do I hope.
My soul waiteth for the Lord more than
they that watch for the morning:
I say, more than they that watch for the morning.
Let Israel hope in the Lord:
for with the Lord there is mercy,
and with Him is plenteous redemption.
And He shall redeem Israel from all his iniquities.

Power of a Praying Nation

WHY DOES A NATION GO TO PRAYER? What can be the motivation behind such a noble endeavor?

Does a nation go to prayer simply to cry out for a respite from the ills that beset her? Is it enough for her to go to prayer only for deliverance from a foreign threat? Do we invoke the name of the Lord only when in peril, hastily going to Him in whatever method appears to bring the most immediate response? If this is our perception of His love and if we believe that this is the purpose for His existence, we are sadly missing the point altogether.

Is our purpose for being here so self indulging? Is our vision so temporal? Is our future so mundane? I think not.

No, we go to the Lord in prayer as a nation not seeking a temporary audience with the Almighty simply to plead our case for personal survival. We go to Him with the knowledge — no, with the conviction — that we are here for a God-ordained purpose. We go to Him because we know that He raised this nation for the well-being of the entire community of nations. We are people of destiny. We have a calling as a nation that rings deep in the hearts of most people.

WE ARE NOT HERE SIMPLY TO PROCREATE, as though our destiny is merely the survival of our species from one generation to the next. We are not wandering aimlessly throughout time, arbitrarily finding ourselves here in this country instead of somewhere else. We are aware. We laugh when we live and we mourn when we die. Each holds in his bosom, no matter how secretly, the understanding, the confession, the hope that he is here for a purpose greater than mere random natural selection.

Unfortunately, it often takes tragedy to re-ignite the outward expression of the inner knowledge of who we really are beyond our humanity, beyond our flesh and blood.

Lesser species have no sense of destiny beyond their need to survive. They are unaware of anything more. In fact, that sense of destiny is the very thing that separates humanity from the rest of God's creation. For us, staying alive is much more than survival; it is much more than instinctively doing what comes naturally. Humanity exists as part of a larger plan, carrying the absolute understanding that there exists above us a power transcending time and space. This power dwells in and passes through a dimension that is truly grasped only by faith and experienced by the humility of prayer and personal confession. More than a power, He is a living, personal, vibrant God who personally loves humanity and covets relationship with them.

So running to Him in panic only when He is needed will not do over the long term. Of course, He will always forgive us and take care of us when we ask Him. The Bible is full of examples of the Lord coming to the aid of His people when they were in great adversity. But there is more to this God than merely 911 calls. He made us because He loves us, because He wants our friendship, because He invested Himself in us for His purposes and plan for humankind. Our destiny is divine in calling and complete in its fulfillment. The need to fulfill one's reason to breathe is the most driving passion in the universe.

Over the long term, being in fellowship with this God on a daily basis makes a whole lot more sense than running to Him, assuming you can find Him, when an emergency arises. This kind of "foul weather friendship" is not what we humans particularly enjoy from one another. Why do we think it is any different with God? He is devoted to a relationship with us based on mutual love and desire.

It is amazing how we think we can go on from one generation to the next, with less and less consideration for the One who made us for His pleasure. We cannot do this thing alone. We cannot survive as a nation (without considering our destiny) by calling to Him as a last resort to all our problems. He is much more exciting as One who unfolds His plan in us daily and strengthens us for the task. He is much more appealing as the One who loves and heals and blesses than as the One who must respond only in a crisis, only to have us forget Him again until the next problem arises.

The self-seeking, self-indulgence of a nation concerned only with its immediate needs denies the greater purpose for our existence. Do we want to merely survive, or do we want to fulfill our reason for being born, in all its wonder and adventure?

LET'S MAKE A DECISION TOGETHER. Let's make the decision to pray for our nation in the times of crisis, as we all want to do. But let us also make the decision to walk circumspectly, serving the God we expect to help us as the One with far more than help for us. He carries in His heart destiny itself—for you, for your children, and for the nation.

"The course of this conflict is not known, yet its outcome is certain. Freedom and fear, justice and cruelty, have always been at war, and we know that God is not neutral between them.

Fellow citizens, we will meet violence with patient justice — assured of the rightness of our cause, and confident of the victories to come. In all that lies before us, may God grant us wisdom, and may He watch over the United States of America."

—President George W. Bush,
Address to the nation September 20, 2001.

Psalm 91

A psalm of confidence in God

He that dwelleth in the secret place of the most High
shall abide under the shadow of the Almighty.
I will say of the Lord,
He is my refuge and my fortress:
my God; in Him will I trust.
Surely He shall deliver thee from the snare of the
fowler, and from the noisome pestilence.
He shall cover thee with His feathers,
and under His wings shalt thou trust:
His truth shall be thy shield and buckler.
Thou shalt not be afraid for the terror by night;
nor for the arrow that flieth by day;
Nor for the pestilence that walketh in darkness;
nor for the destruction that wasteth at noonday.
A thousand shall fall at thy side,
and ten thousand at thy right hand;
but it shall not come nigh thee.
Only with thine eyes shalt thou behold
and see the reward of the wicked.

Because thou hast made the Lord,
which is my refuge,
even the most High, thy habitation;
There shall no evil befall thee,
neither shall any plague come nigh thy dwelling.
For He shall give His angels charge over thee,
to keep thee in all thy ways.
They shall bear thee up in their hands,
lest thou dash thy foot against a stone.
Thou shalt tread upon the lion and adder:
the young lion and the dragon shalt thou trample
under feet.
Because he hath set his love upon me,
therefore will I deliver him:
I will set him on high,
because he hath known My name.
He shall call upon Me,
and I will answer him:
I will be with him in trouble;
I will deliver him, and honor him.
With long life will I satisfy him,
and show him My salvation.

Postscript—

Not One Building Was Left Standing

Michele and Franca Nise arrived in the United States on September 9, 2001, at the invitation of Don and Cathy Nori. They are from a church in Pescara, Italy, where the Noris have centered ministry activities in Italy over the last three years.

Little did the Nises know that they would be here during the most tumultuous time in American history since the attack on Pearl Harbor. The excitement of being here quickly turned to fear as events unfolded on September 11.

Though their scheduled tours were postponed, they were quite content to study the events on television in the relative safety of their mountain retreat.

But something that they did not expect began to happen. Michele and Franca saw a nation rise above fear; they discovered a patriotism in America that they had never experienced. They saw a nation come together in prayer with an absolute resolve to overcome.

To say they were deeply moved by the attack and by our response as a nation, is a gross understatement.

"Something is here that you cannot see on the television. It is like America is a person. This country is alive," was Michele's way of explaining it. The day they left, the Noris gave them their large American flag to take home, because the Nises could not find one to buy. This flag now waves proudly at their home in Pescara, located on the east coast of Italy along the Adriatic Sea.

It should be noted that the Allies, led by American forces, bombed Pescara relentlessly during World War II. Not one building was left standing when the fighting ended. Though the raids were successful in routing the Nazis from their occupation of the city, thousands of innocent people lost their lives by American bombs. To this day, there are heartrending stories of the suffering, the fear, and the death of those terrible days.

Including this bit of history is important here because of the feelings that this Italian couple carry in their hearts towards Americans. The same sentiment is growing all over Europe as a result of what happened in New York and Washington, D.C., on September 11, 2001.

Don Nori received the following e-mail from Michele and Franca immediately after their return home. It is a powerful tribute to how more and more people around the world look at The United States of America.

Dear Pastor Don & Cathy,

"It is difficult to find the words to thank you for all you did during the last two weeks. Everything we desired happened, and usually this happens only in dreams. Thank you for realizing a dream!

"What we have brought back to Italy is not just a testimony; it is like we have received an assignment from God. We feel that our remembrance of what happened is not limited to what we saw or heard on television broadcasts. We have seen another picture.

"In our hearts we now carry a picture, an image, of a strong young man which represents America. We see the strong young man weeping with intense grief because he has been hit in the deepest, unknown parts of his heart.

"We think now that other nations should search again their consciences. Other nations have their physical borders but do not have the same precious treasure that America has. America is like one man.

"We hope to have opportunities to spread out, in the future, what we feel and what we see about America. May all these things carry benefits to other countries like Italy.

God Bless America. We love you."

Michele & Franca.

RECORDING YOUR PERSONAL PRAYERS

As you read this book and begin to pray your own prayers, please use these pages to keep notes about things you have prayed. You should date these items and refer to them often as you pray in the future. It is very encouraging to record how and when God answers your prayers.

_____

_____

_____

_____

_____

_____

_____

_____

_____

_____

_____

_____

_____

_____

_____

The Power of a Praying Nation

_____

_____

_____

_____

_____

_____

_____

_____

_____

_____

_____

_____

_____

_____

_____

_____

_____

_____

_____

_____

_____

_____

_____

_____

_____

_____

_____

_____

_____

_____

_____

_____

_____

_____

_____

_____

_____

_____

_____

_____

_____

_____

_____

_____

_____

_____

_____

_____

_____

_____

_____

_____

_____

_____

_____

_____

_____

_____

_____

_____

_____

_____

_____

_____

_____

_____

_____

_____

_____

_____

_____

_____

The Power of a Praying Nation

_____

_____

_____

_____

_____

_____

_____

_____

_____

_____

_____

_____

_____

_____

_____

_____

_____

_____

_____

_____

_____

_____

_____

_____

_____

_____

_____

_____

_____

_____

_____

_____

_____

_____

_____

Additional copies of this book and other book titles from DESTINY IMAGE are available at your local bookstore.

For a complete list of our titles, visit us at **www.destinyimage.com** Send a request for a catalog to:

Destiny Image® Publishers, Inc.
P.O. Box 310
Shippensburg, PA 17257-0310

"Speaking to the Purposes of God for This Generation and for the Generations to Come"